The XXL Soup Maker Recipe Book

Quick and Delicious Meals For Every Day incl. Desserts and Snacks

Margarete Green

ISBN- 9798495321977

TABLE OF CONTENTS

Introduction

Soup is a great meal choice for not only the cooler months, but for spring and summer too. Depending on the ingredients that you use, a soup can be hearty and warming, or light and refreshing.

Making soup usually involves a lot of chopping and boiling. Yet, by using a soup maker, you can make a variety of soups without issue. In this book, we've compiled more than 40 recipes that you can make in a soup maker, along with a selection of easy-to-make sides to go with your delicious soup.

As a bonus, we've included some breakfast, dessert, and drink recipes that you can make in a soup maker too!

What is a soup maker?

Soup makers are much like blenders or food processors, except that they are usually heated. Whilst a soup maker might not be a kitchen essential, they can save you a great deal of time and effort if you do make soup.

Soup makers can do much more than make soup. Many can also make drinks, smoothies, batters, sauces and more.

Soup makers come in two types, these are jugs and blenders. The jug (or kettle) style soup makers resemble a large kettle and tend to be more affordable. This type of soup maker has the blender attachment in the top of the kettle, which makes it very easy to clean.

Blender style soup makers are usually more expensive than the jug style ones and tend to have extra features such as a sauté function. This type of soup maker looks like a traditional household blender, with the blending tool in the bottom.

Beyond the two types, soup makers can have a range of different capacities and functions. Some brands offer dedicated dessert, smoothie, or sauce functions, for example.

Why use a soup maker?

Soup makers can make light work of so many things, including soups, sauces, smoothies, and more. Without a soup maker, you would need to keep chopping, simmering, and blitzing to create a smooth soup. A soup maker could carry out all these processes for you with ease.

By using a soup maker, you can often save yourself on washing up, and the soup will ready and on the table quicker too. You can also make a big batch of soup with the intention of freezing some for a later date.

Top tips for using a soup maker

Soup makers are a great addition to the kitchen for households who make lots of soups, or those want to start eating soup as part of their diet. Here are a few tips and tricks that will help you to get the most out of the soup maker.

Vegetables

Prepare your ingredients in advance. Make sure that your vegetables are all chopped, peeled, and thawed if needed to make the process of making the soup even easier.

Boiling water

When it comes to making the stock for your soup, use boiling water where possible. Some soup makers may struggle to thoroughly cook the vegetables during their relatively short cycle if you use cold water.

Meat

In the same way, many soup makers do not have a long enough cycle to cook meat through. Unless the soup maker is specifically designed to cook raw meat, always cook your meat before adding it to the soup maker.

Water level

Make sure that the liquid level in your soup maker always falls in between the manufacturer's recommended minimum or maximum lines. If the level is too low, simply top up with extra water or stock.

Safety tips

It is crucial that you take precautions when using a soup maker, as with any kitchen appliance.

Always make sure that the lid is firmly on your soup maker before starting the program, and never open the soup maker during the cooking process.

Keep the soup maker away from the edge of any countertop, especially if you have small children or pets to prevent it from being pulled onto the floor.

Always follow the manufacturer's guidelines as to how to clean the soup maker to avoid damaging the machine or causing it to short out.

How to make soup

Soup is easy to make, whether you are making it by hand or in a soup maker.

The first step is the soup base. Many recipes will start with sautéed onions, and sometimes add carrots, celery, and leeks. These generally need cooking in butter or sweated down before adding further ingredients.

At this stage, you can also add spices and seasonings like salt, pepper, and garlic. If you want a Thai-style soup, include things like garlic, ginger, and coriander. For an Indian flavour, consider spices like cumin, turmeric, and garam masala.

Most recipes will call for somewhere between a pinch and a teaspoon of a given spice. This will give you depth of flavour, without overpowering the rest of your ingredients.

After sweating the vegetables down for your soup's base and adding spices, you can add your main ingredients and stock. The main ingredient could be a vegetable or meat that you want to take centre stage. When it comes to your stock choice, you could use a store-bought stock cube, or make your own.

Once all the ingredients are ready to go, you can make the soup by boiling it on the hob, or by adding all the ingredients to your soup maker. If using a soup maker, you will have the choice of the smooth or chunky setting.

When the soup has finished cooking, serve hot. You can add garnishes, such as spring onions, fresh herbs, and a grind of black pepper.

Essential ingredients of soup

Most soup recipes are flexible and can be adjusted to suit your preferences. For example, you could swap out the vegetables, meats, or stock choices in the recipes in this book to create a soup that suits your tastes. The essential ingredients any soup needs are as follows:

- Broth or stock: you can either use a stock pot or store-bought broth, or make your own by simmering meat scraps and bones

- Vegetables: leftover cooked vegetables, canned vegetables, frozen vegetables, and fresh vegetables all make a great addition to soup

- Canned or dried beans: both can add protein and fibre, and work well in most soup recipes

- Protein: for soups with meat, consider chicken, turkey, or lean beef. For added flavour, you could add sausage, chorizo, or ham. For a vegetarian soup, swap the meat for tofu or an imitation meat

- Herbs and seasonings: herbs like bay leaves, thyme, basil, and oregano all add depth of flavour to most soups. The simple addition of a crushed garlic clove or two can also make the world of difference.

Beyond these, you can also add and subtract ingredients depending on your dietary needs. If you need to eat more protein, for example, you could add extra meat or beans to the soup or serve with a hard-boiled egg. As a variation on a cream-based soup, you can blend in cauliflower or tofu for a creamy texture without the calories.

Soup and weight loss

Soup diets are often touted as being great for weight loss. There are certainly benefits associated with eating soup frequently, regardless of whether you stick to a dedicated soup plan.

By eating soup, especially a homemade one, you can easily consume considerably more vegetables and nutrients than you otherwise would. They are enjoyable and easy to eat, regardless of how many vegetables you squeeze in. Alongside increasing your vegetable intake, soup can also help you increase your water intake.

Soups are filling and yet tend to be very low in calories, especially when compared to foods of a similar weight. This means that eating soup can help you run at a calorie deficit. This will help you lose weight without feeling hungry or dissatisfied after a meal.

Soup also takes longer to eat than some other meals. This gives you more time to enjoy the flavours, and allows your body to feel full, stopping you feeling like you need to eat more than one serving.

Recipes

It is much easier to make a soup, sides, and meals than you might think! In this section, you will find a great range of recipes for soups and ideal sides, along with a range of easy recipes for snacks, breakfasts, and desserts.

We've included a variety of recipes containing meat and others that are vegetarian, and many of the recipes are adaptable to suit different dietary requirements. Some of these recipes can be made in batches to freeze as part of a meal prep plan.

Soup

Our soup recipes are all quick and easy to make with a soup maker. Our selection of recipes includes traditional recipes, vegetarian recipes, exotic recipes and more.

TOMATO AND BASIL SOUP

Tomato and basil soup is a classic choice that is ideal for the coldest winter days.

SERVES 4
PER SERVING: 120 CALORIES, 3.9G PROTEIN, 64G CARBOHYDRATES, 1.6G FAT

INGREDIENTS
- 3 shallots, chopped
- 4 cloves of garlic, crushed
- 5 medium tomatoes, chopped
- 1 medium potato, chopped
- 1 large carrot, peeled and chopped
- 8 basil leaves, chopped
- 800ml // 3.5 cups vegetable stock
- 2 basil leaves, chopped, to garnish

INSTRUCTIONS
1. Add all the ingredients (except basil) to your soup maker. Stir ingredients together. Make sure that you do not go over the MAX line. If you are not above the MIN line, add some hot water to top up.
2. Put the lid on and select the smooth setting.
3. Once the program has finished, take the lid off and add the chopped basil leaves. Blend on the manual setting for about 20 seconds.
4. Garnish with the chopped basil.

APPLE AND PARSNIP SOUP

Apple and parsnip soup is a great hearty choice for autumn dinners.

SERVES 4
PER SERVING: 210 CALORIES, 2.5G PROTEIN, 91G CARBOHYDRATES, 5.6G FAT

INGREDIENTS
- 1 tbsp olive oil
- 2 Granny Smith apples
- 4 parsnips
- 1 tsp ground cinnamon
- 1 onion
- 1 litre // 4 cups vegetable stock

INSTRUCTIONS
1. Peel and chop the apples, parsnips, and onion.
2. Heat the oil in a pan and sauté the onion.
3. Add the ingredients to the soup maker. You may need to top up with a little hot water if the stock does not reach the MIN level. Alternatively, if you would like a thicker soup, add more parsnips and apples.

CHICKEN NOODLE SOUP

Chicken noodle soup is a chunky, hearty soup packed with flavour and vegetables.

SERVES 4
PER SERVING: 319 CALORIES, 24G PROTEIN, 28G CARBOHYDRATES, 12G FAT

INGREDIENTS
- 250g // 9oz chicken, cooked and shredded or diced
- 200g // 7oz potatoes, peeled and cubed
- 70g // 2.5oz carrots, peeled and chopped
- 3 cloves of garlic, crushed
- Juice of 1 lemon
- 100g // 3.5oz egg noodles
- 1 litre // 4 cups chicken stock

INSTRUCTIONS
1. Add all the ingredients to the soup maker, breaking the noodles up as you put them in.
2. Make sure that you do not go over the soup maker's MAX line but top up with more stock or hot water if you are under the MIN line.
3. Put the lid on the soup maker and select the chunky setting.

SPANISH POTATO SOUP

Spanish potato soup is based on a traditional Spanish dish that becomes a great chunky soup.

SERVES 4
PER SERVING: 146 CALORIES, 3.9G PROTEIN, 54G CARBOHYDRATES, 1.2G FAT

INGREDIENTS
- 500g // 17.5oz potatoes, diced
- 1 red onion, sliced
- 4 cloves of garlic, crushed
- 2tsp smoked paprika
- 1tbsp tomato puree
- 1tsp crushed red chillies
- 1 red pepper, chopped, seeds removed
- 1 green pepper, chopped, seeds removed
- 1 tin of chopped tomatoes or passata
- Splash of Tabasco sauce
- 500ml // 2 cups vegetable stock

INSTRUCTIONS

1. Add all the ingredients to the soup maker.
2. Add the vegetable stock, taking care not to go over the MAX line. If needed, top up to the MIN line with vegetable stock.
3. Mix the ingredients together and place the lid on the soup maker.
4. Select the chunky setting.

TOP TIP

Add the tinned tomatoes or passata to the soup maker last so they don't get stuck to the bottom or burn!

Taste the soup as you go and add more or fewer chillies as desired.

MUSHROOM SOUP

Mushroom soup is a comforting choice complete with cream, onions and garlic that makes a great evening meal.

SERVES 4
PER SERVING: 309 CALORIES, 11G PROTEIN, 14G CARBOHYDRATES, 22G FAT

INGREDIENTS
- 90g // 3oz butter
- 2 medium onions, roughly chopped
- 1 garlic clove, crushed
- 500g // 17.5oz mushrooms, finely chopped
- 2 tbsp plain flour
- 1 litre // 4 cups chicken stock
- 4 tbsp cream
- Small handful of flat-leaf parsley to serve

INSTRUCTIONS
1. Heat the butter gently in a large saucepan, and cook the onions and garlic until soft, but not browned. This should take between 8 and 10 minutes.
2. Add the mushrooms and cook on a high heat until softened, and sprinkle over the flour before stirring to combine.
3. Add the contents of the pan to your soup maker and top up with the chicken stock.
4. Set the soup maker on smooth.
5. Once the cycle has finished, stir through the cream, and scatter the parsley over to serve.

BROCCOLI AND STILTON SOUP

Broccoli and stilton are a classic soup flavour combination, made even easier with a soup maker.

SERVES 4
PER SERVING: 275 CALORIES, 16G PROTEIN, 17G CARBOHYDRATES, 14G FAT

INGREDIENTS
- 1 onion, finely chopped
- 1 celery stick, sliced
- 1 leek, sliced
- 1 medium potato, diced
- 750ml // 2 cups chicken or vegetable stock
- 1 head of broccoli, roughly chopped
- 140g // 5oz stilton or other blue cheese, crumbled

INSTRUCTIONS
1. Put all the ingredients in the soup maker, except the stilton and use the smooth soup function.
2. Once the cycle is complete, season to taste, and stir in most of the stilton. Blend briefly to melt the cheese into the soup.
3. Season with black pepper and serve with the reserved cheese on top.

BUTTERNUT SQUASH SOUP

Butternut squash soup is a great autumnal meal and is even better with a sprinkling of chilli.

SERVES 2
PER SERVING: 272 CALORIES, 5G PROTEIN, 28G CARBOHYDRATES, 15G FAT

INGREDIENTS

- 500g // 17.5oz butternut squash, peeled and chopped into cubes
- 1 tsp olive oil
- 1 onion, diced
- 1 small garlic clove, thinly sliced
- 1 mild red chilli, deseeded and finely chopped
- 400ml // 1.5 cups vegetable stock
- 2 tbsp crème fraiche, plus more to serve

INSTRUCTIONS

1. Heat the oven to 200C // 390F. Toss the butternut squash in a roasting tin with the olive oil. Season with salt and pepper, and roast for 30 minutes until golden and softening. Turn the butternut squash once during cooking.
2. Put the roast butternut squash in the soap maker, along with the onion, garlic, most of the chilli, and all the stock.
3. Run the soup maker on the smooth soup function.
4. Once the cycle is complete, season to taste, and add the crème fraiche.
5. Blend briefly on the manual setting until the soup is creamy. Add a little extra stock if you prefer a thinner soup.
6. Serve in bowls with a swirl of crème fraiche and the reserved chopped chilli.

LEEK AND POTATO SOUP

Creamy leek and potato soup is warm and comforting for cold evenings on the sofa.

SERVES 2
PER SERVING: 300 CALORIES, 12G PROTEIN, 24G CARBOHYDRATES, 16G FAT

INGREDIENTS
- 225g // 8oz potatoes, peeled and cut into small cubes
- 1 small onion, diced
- 1 large leek, sliced
- 450ml // 2 cups chicken or vegetable stock
- 60ml // ¼ cup cream, plus a drizzle to serve
- 60ml // ¼ cup full fat milk
- Small knob of butter
- Finely chopped chives

INSTRUCTIONS
1. Put the potatoes, onions, most of the leeks and the stock in the soup maker and use the smooth soup function.
2. Once the cycle has finished, add most of the cream and all the milk and blend briefly. Use the keep warm function whilst you make the topping.
3. Finely shred the remaining leek. Heat the butter in a frying pan, and gently cook the leek until softened but not coloured.
4. Serve the soup in bowls with a drizzle of cream, the cooked leeks, a sprinkling of chives and a couple of cracks of black pepper.

LENTIL, LEEK, AND CARROT SOUP

Not only is this colourful recipe easy to make, but it is also filling and nutritious. It is low in calories too!

SERVES 4
PER SERVING: 103 CALORIES, 6G PROTEIN, 15G CARBOHYDRATES, 1G FAT

INGREDIENTS
- 750ml // 3 cups vegetable or pork stock
- 75g // 2.5oz red lentils
- 3 carrots, finely chopped
- 1 medium leek, sliced
- Small handful of parsley to serve

INSTRUCTIONS
1. Put all the ingredients except the parsley in a soup maker and use the chunky soup function. The soup may look a little foamy to begin with, but this will disappear once the lentils start to cook.
2. At the end of the cycle, check the lentils are cooked and tender, and season to taste. Serve with a scattering of parsley.

ROAST CHICKEN SOUP

Making this soup is a great way to use leftover chicken from a Sunday roast, and it freezes well too!

SERVES 2
PER SERVING: 155 CALORIES, 17G PROTEIN, 8G CARBOHYDRATES, 5G FAT

INGREDIENTS
- 1 onion, chopped
- 1 large carrot, chopped
- 1 tsp thyme leaves, roughly chopped
- 700ml // 3 cups chicken stock
- 100g // 3.5oz frozen peas
- 150g // 5oz leftover roast chicken, shredded
- 1.5 tbsp Greek yogurt
- Small garlic clove, crushed
- Squeeze of lemon juice

INSTRUCTIONS
1. Put the onion, carrots, thyme, stock, and peas in the soup maker, and use the chunky soup function.
2. Once the cycle is complete, stir the shredded roast chicken, and use the soup maker's warm function to heat the chicken.
3. Mix the yogurt, garlic, and lemon juice together.
4. Season the soup and pour into bowls. Serve with a swirl of the yogurt mixture.

CAULIFLOWER SOUP

This delicious soup is comforting and creamy, and the big batch size is ideal for meal prep.

SERVES 4-6
PER SERVING: 176 CALORIES, 8G PROTEIN, 14G CARBOHYDRATES, 8G FAT

INGREDIENTS

- 1 large cauliflower (around 1.5kg // 53oz), cut into florets
- 1 tsp ground cumin
- 2tbsp olive oil, plus extra for drizzling
- 4 sprigs of thyme
- 1 onion, finely chopped
- 1 celery stick, finely chopped
- 1 garlic clove, crushed
- 750ml // 3 cups vegetable or chicken stock
- 100ml // ½ cup cream
- Small bunch of parsley, finely chopped

INSTRUCTIONS

1. Heat the oven to 220C // 420F. Toss the cauliflower in a roasting tin with 1 tbsp of olive oil, the cumin, and the thyme. Roast for 15 minutes until golden and tender. Discard the thyme.

2. Heat the remaining oil in a saucepan with the onion and celery, and fry over a medium heat for 10 minutes until softened. Add the garlic and cook for a further 1 minute.

3. Stir through most of the cauliflower, reserving some to top the soup with.

4. Add the contents of the pan and the stock to the soup maker. Blend the soup on the smooth function.

5. When the cycle finishes, stir through the cream and season to taste. Add extra stock if you would like your soup to be thinner.

6. Ladle the soup into bowls, and top with parsley, the reserved cauliflower, and a drizzle of olive oil.

FRENCH ONION SOUP

French onion soup is rich and easy to make, ideal for cosy nights at home and dinner parties.

SERVES 4
PER SERVING: 618 CALORIES, 26G PROTEIN, 59G CARBOHYDRATES, 27G FAT

INGREDIENTS
- 50g // 1.5oz butter
- 1 tbsp olive oil
- 1kg // 35oz onions, halved and sliced
- 1 tsp sugar
- 4 garlic cloves, thinly sliced
- 2 tbsp flour
- 250ml // 1 cup dry white wine
- 1.3 litres // 5.5 cups of hot, strong beef stock
- 4-8 slices of baguette
- 140g // 5oz gruyère, grated

INSTRUCTIONS

1. Melt the butter with the olive oil over a low heat in a large pan. Add the onions, and fry with the lid on for 10 to 15 minutes until soft.
2. Add the sugar and cook for 20 minutes, stirring regularly until caramelised. Your onions should be golden, flavourful, and soft. Make sure that you stir them regularly to ensure they do not burn.
3. Add the garlic cloves for the last few minutes of cooking time, then add the flour and stir well.
4. Add the wine, cover, and simmer for around 15 minutes.
5. Add the contents to the soup maker, followed by the beef stock and use the chunky setting.
6. Serve the soup in bowls with slices of toasted baguette with a generous serving of the grated gruyère.

MEXICAN TORTILLA SOUP

This comforting soup is made with a Mexican inspired combination of tomatoes, garlic, onions, and chillies.

SERVES 4
PER SERVING: 264 CALORIES, 9.8G PROTEIN, 41.4G CARBOHYDRATES, 6.4G FAT

INGREDIENTS
- 5 cloves of garlic, crushed
- 1 tsp ground cumin
- 1 tin (400g // 14oz) of plum tomatoes
- 1 red chilli, sliced and deseeded
- Juice of 2 limes
- 1 litre // 4 cups of chicken stock
- Tortilla crisps or strips (optional)
- Grated cheese (optional)

INSTRUCTIONS

1. Add the garlic, tomatoes, chilli, lime juice, chicken stock and cumin to your soup maker.
2. Give the mixture a good stir and run the soup maker on the smooth setting.
3. Serve with tortilla crisps or strips, and cheese on top if desired.

TOP TIPS

For a more filling soup, add some shredded chicken. If you want a spicier soup, leave the chilli seeds in!

To make your own tortilla strips, cut up a tortilla wrap into thin slices, brush with a little oil, and cook in the oven at 200C // 390F for 5 minutes.

SPICED ROOT VEGETABLE SOUP

This root vegetable soup is easy to make and affordable, and the addition of spice makes it ideal for cold evenings.

SERVES 4
PER SERVING: 147 CALORIES, 2.9G PROTEIN, 60.3G CARBOHYDRATES, 4.9G FAT

INGREDIENTS
- 1 tbsp olive oil
- 1 small onion
- 2 cloves crushed garlic
- 300g // 10.5oz carrots
- 150g // 5oz parsnips
- 400g // 14oz swede
- 2tsp garam masala
- 700ml // 3 cups vegetable stock (made with 1 cube)

INSTRUCTIONS
1. Peel the vegetables and chop into equal chunks.
2. Heat the oil in a pan, or in the base of the soup maker if it has a sauté function.
3. Add the onion and cook for 2 minutes.
4. Add the garlic and garam masala and cook for a further 2 minutes.
5. Transfer the ingredients from the pan to the soup maker (or switch off the sauté function if used) and add the remaining vegetables and stock.
6. Use the smooth function on the soup maker to finish.

BACON AND LENTIL SOUP

Lentils are a cheap way to make a filling meal, and bacon is just a great addition to just about every dinner.

SERVES 4
PER SERVING: 337 CALORIES, 17.9G PROTEIN, 42.3G CARBOHYDRATES, 10.7G FAT

INGREDIENTS
- 1 tbsp olive oil
- 4 rashers of bacon, fat removed and chopped
- 1 medium onion, diced
- 200g // 7oz red lentils, rinsed thoroughly
- 1 medium potato, diced
- 1 small carrot, diced
- 1 litre // 4 cups chicken stock

INSTRUCTIONS
1. Heat the oil in a pan, or in the base of the soup maker if it has a sauté function and cook the onions and bacon.
2. Add all the ingredients to the soup maker (and switch off the sauté function if using).
3. Set the soup maker on smooth.

THAI RED CURRY NOODLE SOUP

Thai curries are a great warming meal, and what better way to mix it up than as a noodle soup?

SERVES 4
PER SERVING: 349 CALORIES, 18.9G PROTEIN, 14.2G CARBOHYDRATES, 23.9G FAT

INGREDIENTS
- 1 tbsp olive oil
- 300g // 10.5oz chicken
- 2 cloves of garlic
- 1 tbsp grated fresh ginger, or 1tsp ground ginger
- 4-5 tbsp Thai red curry paste
- 1 lemongrass stalk (or zest of half a lemon)
- 2 kaffir lime leaves (or zest of half a lime)
- 1 red chilli, chopped
- 4 spring onions, chopped
- 200ml // ¾ cup coconut milk
- 700ml // 3 cups chicken stock
- 50g dry egg noodles

INSTRUCTIONS

1. Heat the oil in a pan, or in the base of the soup maker if it has a sauté function and cook the garlic and ginger.
2. Turn off the sauté function if using and stir in the red curry paste.
3. If your soup maker cannot take raw meat, chop, and cook the chicken.
4. Add all the ingredients except the noodles to the soup maker, and stir well
5. Set the soup maker on the chunky setting.
6. When the timer has 6 minutes left, add the dry egg noodles and then select the chunky button again. Alternatively, cook the noodles and stir them through the soup at the end of the cycle.

TOP TIPS

If you don't like coconut milk, you can substitute it with natural yoghurt, however the soup may lose some of its sweetness.

JAMAICAN JERK SWEET POTATO SOUP

Sweet potato creates a beautifully smooth soup that is wonderfully warming when combined with chilli and jerk seasoning.

SERVES 4
PER SERVING: 268 CALORIES, 4.6G PROTEIN, 56.3G CARBOHYDRATES, 3.9G FAT

INGREDIENTS
- 600g // 21oz sweet potatoes
- 1 tbsp butter or oil
- 1 onion, sliced
- 2 cloves of garlic, crushed
- 1 red chilli
- 2 tsp Jerk seasoning
- 900ml // 3 ½ cups vegetable stock

INSTRUCTIONS
1. Warm the oil or butter in a pan, and gently sauté the onion and garlic.
2. Add the remaining ingredients.
3. Set the soup maker on the smooth setting.

TOP TIPS

Depending on the type of chilli used, this recipe can be quite hot. If you prefer a milder soup, deseed the chilli first.

MOROCCAN CHICKPEA SOUP

This Moroccan inspired recipe is simple, rich, and so satisfying.

SERVES 3 TO 4
PER SERVING: 432 CALORIES, 21.7G PROTEIN, 72.2G CARBOHYDRATES, 7.3G FAT

INGREDIENTS
- 1 onion, chopped
- 2 garlic cloves, crushed
- 1 carrot, chopped
- 1 celery stalk, chopper
- 400g // 14oz (1 tin) chickpeas, drained and rinsed
- 400g // 14oz (1 tin) chopped tomatoes
- ½ tsp ground cumin
- ½ tsp cinnamon
- ½ tsp paprika
- ½ tsp Cayenne pepper
- 800ml // 3 ¼ cups vegetable stock

INSTRUCTIONS
1. Heat the oil in a pan, or in the base of the soup maker if it has a sauté function, and cook the onion, garlic, and celery.
2. Turn off the sauté function if using and add all the ingredients to the soup maker.
3. Stir the ingredients together and set the soup maker on the smooth setting.
4. (Optional) Garnish with mint leaves to serve.

SPICY TOMATO SOUP

The simple addition of a chilli is enough to give the humble tomato soup a lift.

SERVES 4
PER SERVING: 53 CALORIES, 2G PROTEIN, 15.1G CARBOHYDRATES, 0.5G FAT

INGREDIENTS
- 1 onion, chopped
- 2 cloves garlic, crushed
- 5 fresh tomatoes, quartered
- 1 red chilli, sliced
- 1 tsp grated fresh ginger
- ½ tsp ground cumin
- Vegetable stock (up to the max line)

INSTRUCTIONS
1. Heat the oil in a pan, or in the base of the soup maker if it has a sauté function, and cook the onion, garlic, and ginger.
2. Turn off the sauté function if using and add all the ingredients to the soup maker.
3. Stir the ingredients together and set the soup maker on smooth.
4. (Optional) Top with fresh herbs, a swirl of cream, or grated cheese to serve.

TOP TIPS

Depending on the type of chilli used, this recipe can be quite hot. If you prefer a milder soup, deseed the chilli first.

CARROT AND ORANGE SOUP

It isn't just the colour that makes this soup a great choice for the autumn months. This soup is the perfect combination of sweet carrots and zing from the orange.

SERVES 4
PER SERVING: 114 CALORIES, 2.4G PROTEIN, 24.8G CARBOHYDRATES, 0.7G FAT

INGREDIENTS
- 1 onion, chopped
- 1 clove of garlic
- 500g // 17.5oz carrots
- 1 medium potato
- 300ml // 1 ¼ cups fresh orange juice
- Vegetable stock (up to the max line)
- Seasoning to taste

INSTRUCTIONS
1. Heat the oil in a pan, or in the base of the soup maker if it has a sauté function and cook the onion and garlic.
2. Turn off the sauté function if using and add all the ingredients to the soup maker.
3. Add a vegetable stock pot or cube and top up to the MAX line with hot water.
4. Set the soup maker to smooth and season to taste.
5. (Optional) Stir through crème fraiche to serve.

ASPARAGUS SOUP

Asparagus is easy to prepare and can be cooked in so many ways and can often be made ahead of time. When used in soup, asparagus requires very few additional ingredients to create a satisfying dish.

SERVES 4
PER SERVING: 76 CALORIES, 3.6G PROTEIN, 14.7G CARBOHYDRATES, 0.4G FAT

INGREDIENTS
- 400g // 14oz asparagus, chopped into small pieces
- 1 onion, chopped
- 1 clove of garlic, chopped
- 1 potato, diced
- 2 sticks celery, sliced
- 850ml // 3 ½ cups vegetable stock

INSTRUCTIONS
1. Add all the ingredients to your soup maker, and mix.
2. Set the soup maker on smooth, and season to taste when done.

PRAWN COCKTAIL SOUP

Prawn cocktail soup is a delicate evening meal choice that is diet friendly and so filling.

SERVES 2
PER SERVING: 228 CALORIES, 20G PROTEIN, 17.6G CARBOHYDRATES, 8.6G FAT

INGREDIENTS
- 150g // 5oz cooked king prawns
- 200ml // ¾ cup passata
- 1 onion, diced
- 1 bell pepper, diced
- 1 tbsp grated ginger
- 1 tsp chilli powder
- 1 tsp coriander
- 1 tbsp basil
- 1 tbsp olive oil

INSTRUCTIONS
1. Warm the oil in a pan and sauté the onion and ginger.
2. Add all the ingredients to the soup maker, reserving a few prawns for decoration. Top up with hot water as desired.
3. Blend on the smooth setting.
4. Season to taste and serve with the reserved prawns.

GREEN BEAN AND CARROT SOUP

This easy-to-make soup is ideal for busy weekday nights and happens to be both vegan-friendly and gluten-free too.

SERVES 4
PER SERVING: 162 CALORIES, 3.3G PROTEIN, 15.3G CARBOHYDRATES, 11G FAT

INGREDIENTS
- 1 tbsp olive oil
- 1 onion, chopped
- 2 carrots, peeled and sliced
- 450g // 16oz green beans, trimmed and cut in half
- 500ml // 2 ¼ cups vegetable stock
- 120ml // ½ cup almond milk
- 1 tsp salt
- 1 tsp dried mixed herbs

INSTRUCTIONS
1. Heat the oil in a pan, or in the base of the soup maker if it has a sauté function and cook the onion until translucent.
2. Add the carrots and beans, and sauté for a few minutes.
3. Turn off the sauté setting if using and add all the ingredients to the soup maker.
4. Run the soup maker on the smooth setting, then season to taste.
5. (Optional) Serve with a sprinkling of parsley flakes.

TOMATO AND RED PEPPER SOUP

The sweet flavour of the pepper makes this soup recipe ideal all year round.

SERVES 4
PER SERVING: 142 CALORIES, 3.2G PROTEIN, 16.6G CARBOHYDRATES, 8.1G FAT

INGREDIENTS
- 2 tbsp olive oil
- 1 onion, chopped
- 3 cloves of garlic, sliced
- 750g // 26oz tomatoes, chopped
- 2 red peppers, chopped
- 500ml // 2 ¼ cups vegetable stock
- Handful of basil leaves to serve

INSTRUCTIONS
1. Heat the oil in a pan, or in the base of the soup maker if it has a sauté function and cook the onion and garlic until soft.
2. Turn off the sauté setting if using and add all the ingredients except the basil to the soup maker.
3. Run the soup maker on the smooth setting and serve with a sprinkling of basil.

MEXICAN BEAN SOUP WITH GUACAMOLE

This Mexican inspired soup is warming, full of vegetables, and tastes as good as it looks.

SERVES 2
PER SERVING: 391 CALORIES, 15G PROTEIN, 38G CARBOHYDRATES, 15G FAT

INGREDIENTS
- 2 tsp rapeseed oil
- 1 onion, chopped
- 1 red pepper, chopped
- 2 cloves of garlic, sliced
- 2 tsp mild chilli powder
- 1 tsp ground coriander
- 1 tsp ground cumin
- 400g // 14oz tin chopped tomatoes
- 400g // 14oz tin black beans
- Vegetable stock cube
- 1 small avocado
- Juice of 1 lime

INSTRUCTIONS

1. Heat the oil in a pan, or in the base of the soup maker if it has a sauté function and cook the onion (save 1 tbsp for use later) and pepper until soft.
2. Add the garlic and spices and cook for a few minutes.
3. Turn off the sauté setting if using, and add the contents of the pan, tomatoes, beans, vegetable stock cube and a can of water to the soup maker
4. Run the soup maker on the chunky setting.
5. For the guacamole, peel, and de-stone the avocado and tip into a bowl with the saved onion, coriander, and lime juice, and mash well.
6. Ladle the soup into bowls, and top with the guacamole.

RED PEPPER, SQUASH, AND HARISSA SOUP

Squash and harissa make a comforting soup that's healthy, low in fat, and packed with goodness.

SERVES 6
PER SERVING: 205 CALORIES, 9G PROTEIN, 15G CARBOHYDRATES, 11G FAT

INGREDIENTS

- 700g // 24oz butternut squash, cut into chunks
- 2 red peppers, roughly chopped
- 2 onions, roughly chopped
- 3 tbsp rapeseed oil
- 3 garlic cloves
- 1 tbsp ground coriander
- 2 tsp ground cumin
- 1.2 litres // 5 cups chicken or vegetable stock
- 2 tbsp harissa paste
- 50ml // ¼ cup full fat cream

INSTRUCTIONS

1. Heat the oven to 180C // 350F. Put all the vegetables on a large baking tray and toss with the rapeseed oil, garlic cloves, ground coriander, ground cumin, and a few cracks of black pepper and salt.
2. Roast for 45 minutes until starting to caramelise.
3. Remove from the oven, and squeeze the garlic cloves out of their skins
4. Tip the vegetables into the soup maker, and add the stock, harissa paste, and double cream.
5. Run the soup maker on the smooth setting.
6. Season to taste, and serve with a swirl of harissa if you like.

TOMATO, CHIPOTLE, AND CORN SOUP

This soup is an easy meal with relatively few ingredients and a few spices. You can freeze leftovers for a later date too!

SERVES 4
PER SERVING: 185 CALORIES, 11G PROTEIN, 16G CARBOHYDRATES, 7G FAT

INGREDIENTS

- 1 tbsp rapeseed oil
- 1 onion, finely chopped
- 2 cloves of garlic, chopped
- 2 tsp ground coriander
- Small bunch of fresh coriander leaves
- 400g // 14oz can chopped tomatoes
- 600ml // 2 ½ cups vegetable stock
- 1 tbsp chipotle paste
- 2 corn on the cobs
- 50g // 1 ½oz feta
- 4 tbsp fat-free Greek yoghurt

INSTRUCTIONS

1. Heat the oil in a pan, or in the base of the soup maker if it has a sauté function and cook the onion until starting to soften.
2. Add the garlic and ground coriander and cook for another minute.
3. Turn off the sauté function if using. Add the contents of the pan, tomatoes, stock, and chipotle to the soup maker and run on the smooth setting.
4. Meanwhile, cook the corn in boiling water for 4 minutes. Drain, and leave to cool.
5. Cut the corn kernels off with a sharp knife and heat a frying pan over a high heat. Fry the corn for around 5 minutes, until charred.
6. Dish the soup into bowls, and serve with a swirl of yogurt, crumbled feta, the charred corn, and coriander leaves.

COURGETTE, LEEK, AND GOAT'S CHEESE SOUP WITH RYE

This healthy soup is packed with flavour, low in calories, and contains three of your five-a-day.

SERVES 4
PER SERVING: 304 CALORIES, 16G PROTEIN, 20G CARBOHYDRATES, 16G FAT

INGREDIENTS

- 1 tbsp rapeseed oil
- 400g // 14oz leeks, washed and sliced
- 450g // 16oz courgettes, sliced
- 400g // 14oz spinach
- 150g // 5 ½oz soft goat's cheese
- 15g // ½oz basil, plus extra to serve
- 1 litre // 4 cups vegetable stock
- 4x 25g // ¾oz portions of wholegrain rye bread

INSTRUCTIONS

1. Heat the oil in a pan, or in the base of the soup maker if it has a sauté function and cook the leeks until starting to soften. Add the courgettes, then cook for a further 5 minutes.
2. Turn off the sauté function if using. Add the contents of the pan, the stock, spinach, and basil leaves to the soup maker and run the smooth cycle.
3. Add the goat's cheese, and blend for a couple of minutes to incorporate.
4. Serve with a sprinkling of basil leaves and the rye bread.

CURRIED KALE AND CHICKPEA SOUP

This soup is budget friendly, healthy, and packed full of vegetables and great flavours.

SERVES 2
PER SERVING: 336 CALORIES, 16G PROTEIN, 40G CARBOHYDRATES, 10G FAT

INGREDIENTS
- 1 tsp rapeseed or coconut oil
- 1 onion, chopped
- 1 tbsp grated ginger
- 2 cloves of garlic, crushed
- 200g // 7oz sweet potato, peeled and cut into cubes
- 1 tsp turmeric
- 2 tsp ground cumin
- 2 tbsp medium or hot curry powder
- 400g // 14oz tin of chickpeas, rinsed
- 150ml // ¾ cup coconut milk
- 500ml // 2 cups vegetable stock
- 160g // 5 ½oz kale, chopped
- Juice of 1 lime
- 1 red chilli (optional)

INSTRUCTIONS

1. Heat the oil in a pan, or in the base of the soup maker if it has a sauté function and cook the onions until starting to soften. Add the ginger and garlic and cook for a minute more.
2. Add all the ingredients excluding the lime and chilli to the soup maker and stir well.
3. Run the soup maker on smooth, and serve with a squeeze of lime juice and, if you like, the chilli slices.

LEEK AND BUTTER BEAN SOUP WITH KALE AND BACON

This dairy free soup has a creamy texture, is nutritious and comforting.

SERVES 4
PER SERVING: 274 CALORIES, 14G PROTEIN, 21G CARBOHYDRATES, 12G FAT

INGREDIENTS
- 4 tsp olive oil
- 500g // 17oz leeks, sliced
- 4 thyme sprigs, leaves only
- 2x 400g // 14oz cans of butter beans
- 500ml // 2 cups vegetable stock
- 2 tsp wholegrain mustard
- Bunch of flat-leaf parsley
- 3 rashers of bacon
- 40g // 1 ½oz kale, chopped
- 25g // 1oz hazelnuts, roughly chopped

INSTRUCTIONS

1. Heat 1 tbsp oil in a pan, or in the base of the soup maker if it has a sauté function and cook the leeks and thyme until softened. Add a splash of water if the leeks start to stick.
2. Add the leeks, butter beans, stock, and mustard to the soup maker, and blend on the smooth setting.
3. Season to taste and stir through the parsley.
4. Meanwhile, fry the bacon until crispy over a medium heat, then set aside to cool.
5. Add the remaining teaspoon of oil to the pan, and tip in the kale and hazelnuts. Cook for 2 minutes until the kale wilts and starts to crisp at the edges and the hazelnuts are toasted. Cut the bacon into small pieces and add to the pan.
6. Serve the soup in bowls sprinkled with the bacon and kale mixture.

RED LENTIL AND CHORIZO SOUP

This recipe combines smoked paprika and cumin to create a rustic soup.

SERVES 6
PER SERVING: 260 CALORIES, 18G PROTEIN, 16G CARBOHYDRATES, 13G FAT

INGREDIENTS
- 1 tbsp olive oil, plus extra to drizzle
- 200g // 7oz cooking chorizo, peeled, and diced
- 1 large onion, chopped
- 2 carrots, chopped
- Pinch of cumin seeds
- 3 garlic cloves, chopped
- 1 tsp smoked paprika, plus extra for sprinkling
- Pinch of golden caster sugar
- Small splash red wine vinegar
- 250g // 8 ¾oz red lentils
- 2 x 400g // 14oz cans chopped tomatoes
- 850ml // 3 ½ cups chicken stock
- Plain yogurt to serve

INSTRUCTIONS

1. Heat the oil in a pan and cook the chorizo until crisp. Remove with a slotted spoon, leaving the oil in the pan.
2. Fry the onions, carrots, and cumin seeds in the chorizo oil until soft, then add the garlic and fry for a minute more.
3. Add the contents of the pan, the paprika, sugar, vinegar, lentils, tomatoes, and chicken stock to the soup maker, and run the chunky setting.
4. Serve in bowls drizzled with olive oil, yogurt, chorizo, and a sprinkling of paprika.

BROCCOLI, GRUYÈRE, AND CHORIZO SOUP

The spicy sausage and cheese make for a satisfying winter soup.

SERVES 6
PER SERVING: 392 CALORIES, 26G PROTEIN, 7G CARBOHYDRATES, 28G FAT

INGREDIENTS
- 1 tbsp mustard seeds
- 1 tbsp fennel seeds
- 150g // 5 ½oz chorizo, cut into cubes
- 1 tbsp rapeseed oil
- 1 onion, chopped
- 2 garlic cloves, chopped
- 1 ½ litres // 6 ½ cups chicken stock
- 800g // 28oz broccoli, cut into florets
- 150g // 5 ½oz gruyère, grated
- 3 tbsp full fat cream

INSTRUCTIONS

1. Fry the mustard and fennel seeds in a dry pan over a medium heat until the mustard seeds start to pop. Using a pestle and mortar, grind the seeds to a fine powder.
2. In a large saucepan, fry the chorizo (without any oil) for 4 minutes over a medium heat until it releases its oils, then use a slotted spoon to transfer it to a plate and set aside.
3. Add the oil, onion, and garlic to the pan. Cook for 10 minutes until the onion softens. Stir in the spice mix and cook for a further minute.
4. Add the broccoli, chicken stock and contents of the pan to the soup maker and use the smooth function.
5. Season to taste and stir in the cream and two thirds of the cheese.
6. Spoon into bowls and serve with the remaining cheese and chorizo.

PORTUGUESE TOMATO SOUP WITH POACHED EGGS

For a continental meal, try this Portuguese tomato soup served with poached eggs.

SERVES 4
PER SERVING: 192 CALORIES, 11G PROTEIN, 25G CARBOHYDRATES, 10.9G FAT

INGREDIENTS
- 1 onion
- 1 tbsp olive oil
- 2 cloves of garlic
- 1 leek, sliced
- 7 ripe tomatoes
- 1 tbsp tomato puree
- 1.3L // 5½ cups vegetable stock
- 6 eggs

INSTRUCTIONS
1. Add all the ingredients apart from the eggs to the soup maker. Season to taste.
2. Blend the soup on the smooth function.
3. Transfer the blended soup into a large pan at a medium heat, add the eggs, and allow to poach for between 4 and 7 minutes.

MINTY PEA AND POTATO SOUP

This vibrant soup has a fresh taste and is substantial enough for an evening meal.

SERVES 4
PER SERVING: 249 CALORIES, 11G PROTEIN, 48G CARBOHYDRATES, 3G FAT

INGREDIENTS
- 2 tsp vegetable oil
- 1 onion, chopped
- 800g // 28oz potatoes, peeled and cut into small chunks
- 1L // 4 cups vegetable stock
- 350g // 12oz frozen peas
- Handful mint leaves, chopped

INSTRUCTIONS
1. Heat the oil in a large saucepan, then fry the onion for 5 mins until softened.
2. Add the potatoes, stock, and onions to the soup maker, and use the smooth function.
3. Add the peas, then blend using the manual function for a couple minutes.
4. Season with salt and pepper to taste and serve sprinkled with the chopped mint.

CARROT AND CORIANDER SOUP

This soup is luxurious, tasty, and has a creamy finish.

SERVES 3-4
PER SERVING: 182 CALORIES, 3.6G PROTEIN, 30.7G CARBOHYDRATES, 5.3G FAT

INGREDIENTS
+ 1 tsp olive oil
+ 200ml // ¾ cups cream
+ 1 tsp ground coriander
+ 800ml // 3½ cups hot water
+ 1 vegetable or chicken stock pot
+ 600g // 21oz carrots, peeled and sliced
+ 1 onion, chopped
+ 75g // 2½oz potatoes, sliced

INSTRUCTIONS
1. Sauté the onions in the olive oil, adding your stock pot as the onions soften.
2. In the pot, add your onion mix, and the rest of your ingredients. Make sure to stir well before switching it on. It really does help to avoid soup sticking to the base of your soup maker if you don't have a non-stick surface.
3. Select the smooth function for this option.
4. Serve with croutons.

WINTER VEGETABLE SOUP

This soup is a great way to use leftover vegetables.

SERVES 4-6
PER SERVING: 172 CALORIES, 2.8G PROTEIN, 18.6G CARBOHYDRATES, 10.4G FAT

INGREDIENTS
- 1 red onion
- 150g // 5¼oz leeks, chopped
- 100g //3½oz carrots, sliced
- 100g //3½oz swede or turnips, chopped
- 200g // 7oz baby potatoes, washed and peeled
- 50g // 1¾oz butter
- 1 chicken stock pot
- 800ml // 3½cups boiling water

INSTRUCTIONS
1. Sauté your onions and leek for a couple of minutes, until they're soft, but still light in colour.
2. Add all your ingredients to the pot, stir well and select the smooth function setting.
3. Serve hot with fresh bread.

TOP TIP

If you prefer a chunky soup, just use the chunky function instead!

PICKLED ONION AND CELERY SOUP

Pickled onions have a strong flavour, but if you like a tangy taste, give this soup a go.

SERVES 4-6
PER SERVING: 225 CALORIES, 3.6G PROTEIN, 35.9G CARBOHYDRATES, 13.7G FAT

INGREDIENTS
+ 150g // 5oz small, pickled onions, drained
+ 150g // 5oz celery, chopped
+ 150g // 5oz potatoes, cubed
+ 150g // 5oz carrots, sliced
+ 800ml // 3½cups vegetable stock
+ 1 tbsp olive oil

INSTRUCTIONS
1. Lightly sauté the pickled onions in some olive oil. The goal is to release the pickled onion taste, without the onions becoming brown or overcooked.
2. Add all the ingredients into your soup maker and choose the chunky setting.
3. Serve chunky, or blend if you prefer your soup smooth, but the tangy oniony taste that you can get with the chunky version will fade into the other vegetables when they're pureed.

TOP TIP

Use onions picked in a sweet vinegar for a less tangy taste.

SOYA BEAN AND ONION SOUP

This bold soup is packed with flavour and makes a great evening meal when it's cold out.

SERVES 4-6
PER SERVING: 172 CALORIES, 2.8G PROTEIN, 18.6G CARBOHYDRATES, 10.4G FAT

INGREDIENTS
◆ 300g // 10½oz soya beans
◆ 300g // 10½oz onions, finely sliced
◆ 200g // 7oz potatoes, peeled and chopped
◆ 800ml // 3½oz vegetable stock
◆ 1 tsp cardamom powder
◆ 1 tsp olive oil

INSTRUCTIONS
1. Lightly sauté the onions and cardamom with a pinch of salt and pepper, in the olive oil.
2. Add all the ingredients to the soup maker and stir very well.
3. Choose the smooth setting for a thick soup.
4. Season to taste.

CREAM OF SWEET POTATO SOUP

Sweet potatoes make a great soup that is packed with flavour and pairs well with spices.

SERVES 4-6
PER SERVING: 196 CALORIES, 3.6G PROTEIN, 34.4G CARBOHYDRATES, 5.2G FAT

INGREDIENTS
- 100g // 3½oz leeks, sliced
- 50g // 1¾oz onion, sliced
- 550g // 19½oz sweet potato, chopped
- 1 tbsp rapeseed oil
- 1 tsp salt
- 1 tsp ground pepper
- 2 vegetable stock cubes
- 1 tsp turmeric
- 1 tsp paprika
- 1 tsp nigella seeds
- 1 star anise
- Half a lemon
- Water to top up
- 100ml // ½ cup cream (optional)

INSTRUCTIONS

1. Sauté the leek and onion with the salt in the rapeseed oil.
2. Add all the other ingredients to the pot, apart from the lemon and the cream.
3. Select the chunky setting. At the end of the program, remove the star anise and blend again for a smooth soup.
4. When the soup is finished, squeeze in the lemon juice of half a lemon.
5. If you are freezing any of this recipe, do so before adding any cream.

PEPPERED MUSHROOM SOUP

Mushrooms make for a great soup, all year round. Combine with leeks and cracked pepper for a hearty finish.

SERVES 4-6
PER SERVING: 158 CALORIES, 7.5G PROTEIN, 13.7G CARBOHYDRATES, 9.4G FAT

INGREDIENTS
- 400g // 14oz mushrooms, washed and chopped
- 200g // 7oz leeks, chopped
- 1 onion, chopped
- 1L // 4 cups beef stock
- 1 tsp ground peppercorns
- Double cream to serve

INSTRUCTIONS
1. Add your chopped mushrooms, leeks, and onions to the soup maker.
2. Add in a pinch of salt, the ground peppercorns, and the stock up to the max line.
3. Set to the smooth setting.
4. Serve with a little cream to temper the slightly spicy taste of the peppercorns and decorate with some chopped chives.

COCONUT AND LIME SOUP

This recipe is hearty and warming and is a great way to use up leftover potatoes.

SERVES 4-6
PER SERVING: 322 CALORIES, 4.7G PROTEIN, 29.5G CARBOHYDRATES, 22.6G FAT

INGREDIENTS
- 300g // 10oz potatoes, cubed
- 150g // 5oz carrots, chopped
- 75g // 2½oz onions, finely chopped
- 200g // 3½oz leeks, chopped
- 50ml // ¼ cup lime juice
- 350ml // 1½ cups coconut milk
- 350ml // 1½ cups chicken stock
- ½ tsp ground ginger
- 1 tsp olive oil

INSTRUCTIONS
1. Sauté the leak and onion until the onions are soft.
2. Add all the ingredients to the soup maker and run the smooth program.
3. Serve with basil or grated lime zest.

BONUS: Making stock in your soup maker

Most soup recipes will call for the addition of stock, and most people will reach for a store-bought one. Fresh stock will always result in a better flavour than store bought stock, and fortunately, this is something you can make in the soup maker itself.

INGREDIENTS
+ Bones or leftover meat from your chosen protein
+ Hot water

OPTIONAL INGREDIENTS
+ Salt and pepper
+ Garlic
+ Onions

INSTRUCTIONS
1. Add all your ingredients to the soup maker and fill with hot water up to at least the MIN line.
2. Run the chunky cycle.
3. If you like a stronger stock, run the chunky cycle a second time.
4. Once the stock is ready, sieve the liquid to remove the bones and meat from the stock. The stock is now either ready to use, or you can freeze the stock for a later date.

Soup Sides

If you want to make your soup a filling dinner, you want to serve it alongside a side dish, such as a bread or salad. All our soup sides are quick and easy to make, using as few ingredients as possible.

EASY GARLIC BREAD

This simple garlic bread uses a store-bought loaf, and so will be ready in just a few minutes.

SERVES 8

PER SERVING: 195 CALORIES, 6.2G PROTEIN, 27G CARBOHYDRATES, 7G FAT

INGREDIENTS

◆ 1 loaf French bread, or other medium-sized loaf

◆ 4 tablespoons melted butter

◆ 3 cloves of garlic, grated

◆ 1 tablespoon finely chopped parsley

◆ 2 tablespoons parmesan cheese

◆ Pinch of salt

INSTRUCTIONS

1. Pre-heat the oven to 200C // 400F.
2. Slice the loaf of bread in half lengthwise.
3. Mix the butter with the finely chopped parsley and grated garlic, then brush the garlic butter onto the cut sides of the bread. Sprinkle with the salt.
4. Place the cut sides of the bread halves together and wrap the loaf in foil. Place the bread on a baking sheet and bake for 8 minutes until warmed through.
5. Remove the foil and place the bread cut side up on the baking sheet. Sprinkle with grated Parmesan cheese.
6. Cook for a further few minutes until browned and crispy.

SPINACH SALAD WITH BACON DRESSING

When it comes to sides that are flavourful yet relatively healthy, you cannot go wrong with a spinach and bacon salad.

SERVES 6
PER SERVING: 97 CALORIES, 2G PROTEIN, 8G CARBOHYDRATES, 7G FAT

INGREDIENTS

- 400g // 14oz torn fresh spinach
- 3 bacon strips, diced
- 1 red onion, chopped
- 2 tablespoons brown sugar
- 2 tablespoons cider vinegar
- ¼ tsp salt
- ¼ tsp ground mustard seeds
- ¼ tsp celery seeds
- ¼ tsp pepper
- 1 tsp cornflour or cornstarch
- 80ml // ⅓ cup cold water

INSTRUCTIONS

1. Place spinach in a large salad bowl; set aside. In a small non-stick pan, cook bacon over medium heat until crisp. Using a slotted spoon, remove to paper towels to drain.
2. In the same pan, sauté the onion until tender. Stir in the brown sugar, vinegar, salt, mustard seeds, celery seeds and pepper.
3. Combine cornflour and water until smooth and stir into the pan. Bring to a boil; cook and stir until thickened.
4. Remove from the heat; pour over spinach and toss to coat. Sprinkle with bacon.

ROASTED PARMESAN AND ROSEMARY POTATOES

If you like a side with more bite, our roasted parmesan and rosemary potatoes are easy, light, and oh-so-tasty.

SERVES 4
PER SERVING: 233 CALORIES, 5.2G PROTEIN, 27.7G CARBOHYDRATES, 12.2G FAT

INGREDIENTS
- 3 tbsp olive oil
- 2 tbsp grated parmesan
- 1 tbsp fresh chopped rosemary
- 700g // 25oz new potatoes, cut into small cubes

INSTRUCTIONS
1. Preheat the oven to 220C // 425F and line a baking tray with foil.
2. Mix the potatoes, olive oil, parmesan and rosemary in a bowl, and season to taste.
3. Tip the potatoes into the prepared tray and spread out evenly.
4. Bake for 40 minutes until golden and tender, turning once during cooking.

CHEESY CAULIFLOWER BREADSTICKS

This side is packed with cheese and using cauliflower instead of flour means it's gluten free.

MAKES 12 BREADSTICKS
PER BREADSTICK: 66 CALORIES, 5 G PROTEIN, 4G CARBOHYDRATES, 4G FAT

INGREDIENTS
- 1 medium cauliflower
- 100g // 3.5oz mozzarella, shredded
- 50g // 1 ¾oz parmesan, grated
- 50g // 1 ¾oz cheddar, grated
- 1 large egg
- 2 tbsp fresh basil, chopped
- 2 tbsp fresh parsley, chopped
- 1 garlic clove, crushed

INSTRUCTIONS

1. Preheat the oven to 220C // 425F. Process the cauliflower in batches in a food processor until finely ground.
2. Microwave covered in a bowl until tender, this should take about 8 minutes. Once the cauliflower is cool enough to handle, wrap in a clean towel and squeeze dry.
3. In a bowl, mix the cheeses together and stir half of the mix into the cauliflower. Add the herbs, garlic, egg, and season to taste.
4. Line a tray with baking paper and shape the cauliflower mixture into a rectangle. Bake until the edges turn golden, around 20-25 minutes.
5. Top with the reserved cheese and bake for a further 10-12 minutes until melted.
6. Cut into 12 breadsticks to serve.

AVOCADO SALAD

This delightful salad is light and full of crisp, fresh vegetables.

SERVES 2
PER SERVING: 176 CALORIES, 3G PROTEIN, 14G CARBOHYDRATES, 13G FAT

INGREDIENTS
- 1 tomato, cut into eighths
- 1 small cucumber, sliced
- 1 red onion, halved and sliced thinly
- 1 bell pepper, sliced
- 2 tbsp Italian salad dressing
- 1 ripe avocado, peeled and cubed

INSTRUCTIONS
1. Combine the tomato, cucumber, onion, and pepper in a bowl, and toss with the salad dressing.
2. Chill until ready to serve.
3. Add the avocado cubes just before serving.

Breakfast

The soup maker can do a great job at whipping up nutritious food in the morning when you are in a rush. Making delicious breakfasts doesn't need to be time consuming or complicated!

HOT CHOCOLATE BREAKFAST SMOOTHIE

This hot chocolate breakfast smoothie is ideal for cold mornings or if you just fancy a little treat.

SERVES 2
PER SERVING: 569 CALORIES, 7.8G PROTEIN, 41G CARBOHYDRATES, 44G FAT

INGREDIENTS
- 60g // 2oz oats
- 4 medjool dates, pitted
- 2 tbsp nut butter
- 250ml // 1 cup boiled water
- 400g // 14oz can of coconut milk
- 40g // 1 ½oz dark chocolate
- 2 tsp vanilla extract
- Pinch of sea salt

INSTRUCTIONS
1. Add the oats and medjool dates to the soup maker. Add the freshly boiled water and leave to steep for 5 minutes to soften the ingredients.
2. Add the remaining ingredients, secure the lid, and use the manual blend function for a minute to incorporate the ingredients.
3. Cook the mixture using the smooth function for a few minutes, then blend using the manual function for a few more minutes before serving.

BANANA SMOOTHIE

If your soup maker has either a smoothie function or simply one that isn't heated, this smoothie recipe is a great addition to your morning.

SERVES 4
PER SERVING: 231 CALORIES, 7.9G PROTEIN, 37G CARBOHYDRATES, 6.7G FAT

INGREDIENTS
- 400g // 14oz bananas
- 700ml // 3 cups milk
- 150g // 5 ¼oz vanilla ice cream

INSTRUCTIONS
1. Place all the ingredients in the soup maker and use the smoothie function.
2. Once ready, serve in tall glasses with a straw.

MATCHA GRIES

This smooth porridge is a great breakfast served with fruit that's easy to whip up.

SERVES 2
PER SERVING: 231 CALORIES, 7.9G PROTEIN, 37G CARBOHYDRATES, 6.7G FAT

INGREDIENTS
- 450ml // 2 cups milk
- 70g // 2.5oz semolina
- ½ tsp matcha powder
- 2 tbsp honey
- 1 tsp vanilla

INSTRUCTIONS
1. Add all the ingredients to the soup maker.
2. Use the smooth soup function.
3. Serve immediately garnished with your choice of fresh fruit or nuts.

STRAWBERRY AND PINEAPPLE SMOOTHIE

This smooth, refreshing fruit smoothie is a great way to start your day with a couple servings of fruit.

SERVES 4
PER SERVING: 130 CALORIES, 1.3G PROTEIN, 33G CARBOHYDRATES, 0.4G FAT

INGREDIENTS
- 300g // 10½oz frozen strawberries
- 400g // 14oz pineapple chunks
- 1 banana, sliced
- 250ml //1 cup orange juice

INSTRUCTIONS
1. Place all the ingredients in the soup maker and use the smoothie function.
2. Once ready, serve in tall glasses with a straw.

BLUEBERRY AND OAT SMOOTHIE

Blueberries give this smoothie a refreshing taste that is a delicious addition to a morning routine.

SERVES 4
PER SERVING: 300 CALORIES, 15.1G PROTEIN, 46G CARBOHYDRATES, 7.1G FAT

INGREDIENTS
◆ 800g // 28oz low fat natural yoghurt
◆ 400ml milk
◆ 60g // 2oz oats
◆ 150g // 5½oz blueberries
◆ 3 tbsp honey

INSTRUCTIONS
1. Place all the ingredients in the soup maker and use the smoothie function.
2. Once ready, serve in tall glasses with a straw.

CHOCOLATE AND BANANA SMOOTHIE

For those with a sweet tooth, you cannot go wrong with the combination of chocolate and banana.

SERVES 4
PER SERVING: 365 CALORIES, 14.3G PROTEIN, 54.5G CARBOHYDRATES, 10.6G FAT

INGREDIENTS
- 800g // 28oz low fat vanilla yoghurt
- 2 ripe bananas, sliced
- 300ml // 1¼ cups milk
- 200g // 7oz dark chocolate

INSTRUCTIONS
1. Melt the chocolate in a microwave or over a pan of water.
2. Place all the ingredients in the soup maker and use the smoothie function until the desired consistency is achieved.
3. Once ready, serve in tall glasses with a straw.

GREEN SMOOTHIE

This smoothie recipe is flavourful and packed with nutrients.

SERVES 4
PER SERVING: 94 CALORIES, 1.6G PROTEIN, 23.7G CARBOHYDRATES, 0.4G FAT

INGREDIENTS
- 50g // 1¾oz spinach
- 50g // 1¾oz carrots
- 100g // 3½oz cucumber
- 100g // 3½oz pear
- 100g // 3½oz kiwi
- 50g // 1¾oz kale
- 160g // 5½oz apples
- 50ml // ¼ cup lemon juice
- 50ml // ¼ cup lime juice
- 750ml // 3 cups water

INSTRUCTIONS
1. Add all the ingredients to your soup maker.
2. Use the manual blend function on the blender to blend on and off until it reaches your desired consistency.

PEACH AND ORANGE SMOOTHIE

Using canned peaches makes this recipe just as flavourful, but even easier.

SERVES 4
PER SERVING: 133 CALORIES, 2.4G PROTEIN, 31.6G CARBOHYDRATES, 0.5G FAT

INGREDIENTS
- 400g // 14oz can of peaches, including juice
- 400g // 14oz oranges, peeled and sliced
- 600ml // 2 ½ cups orange juice

INSTRUCTIONS
1. Drain peaches, keeping the juice for later.
2. Add peaches and oranges to the soup maker or blender with the orange juice and blend until completely smooth.
3. Add a little of the peach juice at a time, until the drink is at the thickness you like.

MANGO, PINEAPPLE, APPLE, AND PASSION FRUIT SMOOTHIE

This refreshing smoothie is a great way to get four portions of fruit in the morning.

SERVES 4
PER SERVING: 164 CALORIES, 2.7G PROTEIN, 41.5G CARBOHYDRATES, 0.8G FAT

INGREDIENTS
- 200g // 7oz oranges, peeled and sliced
- 200g // 7oz mango, chopped
- 200g // 7oz passion fruit, peeled and diced
- 500g // 17½oz pineapple, peeled and diced
- 500g // 17½oz crushed ice

INSTRUCTIONS
1. Peel and chop the fruit roughly.
2. Put all the fruit and crushed ice into your machine and blend until smooth.
3. Add some ice into a glass and pour the smoothie on top to keep it extra cold.

STRAWBERRY, PEACH, AND PEAR SMOOTHIE

This smoothie recipe is one that will be enjoyed by all the family.

SERVES 4
PER SERVING: 133 CALORIES, 2.1G PROTEIN, 33.1G CARBOHYDRATES, 0.7G FAT

INGREDIENTS
◆ 600g // 21oz crushed ice
◆ 200g // 7oz strawberries
◆ 400g // 14oz peaches
◆ 400g // 14oz pears

INSTRUCTIONS
1. Chop and peal all the ingredients.
2. Add all ingredients to the soup maker.
3. Stir to mix ice and fruit before putting on the lid.
4. Switch on blender function and let it run for a minute.
5. Check your smoothie an stir a little if the ice stops crunching up, or if you prefer your smoothie more blended.
6. Serve immediately.

Snacks

These next few recipes are all light soup ideas that are packed with flavour but low in calories. They would make a great mid-afternoon snack or can be easily made into a small lunch too.

TOMATO AND CABBAGE SOUP

This cabbage soup is low in calories and so makes a great light lunch or snack.

SERVES 4
PER SERVING: 90 CALORIES, 3.6G PROTEIN, 22.6G CARBOHYDRATES, 0.6G FAT

INGREDIENTS
- 1 onion, chopped
- 2 cloves of garlic
- 1 cabbage
- 1 bell pepper, chopped
- 400g // 14oz tin of chopped tomatoes
- 1 tsp dried mixed herbs
- 700ml // 3 cups vegetable stock

INSTRUCTIONS
1. Remove the leaves from the cabbage and shred.
2. Add all the ingredients to the soup maker, making sure to stay below the MAX line. The cabbage leaves will start to squash down when stock is poured on top.
3. Give the ingredients a stir and set the soup maker off on the chunky setting.
4. Season to taste with salt and pepper.

CARROT AND GINGER SOUP

This soup is low fat and warming, ideal for a small lunch or light snack.

SERVES 4
PER SERVING: 293 CALORIES, 10G PROTEIN, 31G CARBOHYDRATES, 12G FAT

INGREDIENTS
- 1 tbsp rapeseed oil
- 1 onion, chopped
- 2 tbsp grated ginger
- 2 cloves of garlic, sliced
- ½ tsp ground nutmeg
- 850ml // 3 ½ cups vegetable stock
- 500g // 17oz carrots, sliced
- 400g // 14oz tin of cannellini beans
- 4 tbsp almonds (optional)

INSTRUCTIONS
1. Heat the oil in a pan, or in the base of the soup maker if it has a sauté function and cook the onions, ginger, and garlic until starting to soften. Add the nutmeg and stir together.
2. Add all the ingredients to the soup maker and run on the chunky setting.
3. Serve with slivers of almonds if you like.

BROCCOLI, CAULIFLOWER, AND CARROT SOUP

This soup can be easily customised depending on your tastes and is a quick and easy lunch or snack.

SERVES 3
PER SERVING: 60 CALORIES, 2.8G PROTEIN, 19G CARBOHYDRATES, 0.4G FAT

INGREDIENTS

- 500g carrot, cauliflower, and broccoli, chopped
- Vegetable stock cube
- Salt and pepper to taste
- Hot water

INSTRUCTIONS

1. Put all the vegetables in the soup maker.
2. Add salt and pepper to taste, and sprinkle in the stock cube.
3. Fill the soup maker to the MIN level, and switch on the smooth setting.

PEA AND HAM SOUP

The traditional combination of pea and ham makes for an easy snack or light evening meal offering two of your five-a-day.

SERVES 4
PER SERVING: 260 CALORIES, 24G PROTEIN, 24G CARBOHYDRATES, 6G FAT

INGREDIENTS
+ 1 onion, chopped
+ 1 medium potato, peeled and diced
+ 1 litre // 4 cups of pork stock
+ 500g // 17.5oz frozen peas or petit pois
+ 300g // 10oz thick sliced ham, trimmed of fat and diced

INSTRUCTIONS
1. Put the onion, potatoes, peas, and stock into a soup maker and use the smooth function.
2. When the cycle finishes, season to taste, and stir through the diced ham before serving.

PUMPKIN SOUP

Pumpkin soup is an easy meal to whip up as a snack, a starter for a dinner party, or as an easy meal in the autumn months.

SERVES 6
PER SERVING: 317 CALORIES, 6G PROTEIN, 20G CARBOHYDRATES, 0.5G FAT

INGREDIENTS

- 2 tbsp olive oil
- 2 onions, chopped
- 1kg // 35oz pumpkin, peeled, deseeded, and chopped
- 700ml // 3 cups vegetable or chicken stock
- 150ml // ¾ cup full fat cream

INSTRUCTIONS

1. Heat the oil in a pan, or in the base of the soup maker if it has a sauté function and cook the onion until soft but not coloured.
2. Add the pumpkin and cook until starting to soften.
3. Turn off the sauté setting if using and add all the ingredients apart from the cream to the soup maker.
4. Run the soup maker on smooth, then add the cream and mix again for a few minutes.

BEETROOT AND ONION SEED SOUP

This soup is quick and easy to make, with a deep, autumnal colour that's full of flavour, low in fat, and vegetarian.

SERVES 1
PER SERVING: 257 CALORIES, 12G PROTEIN, 41G CARBOHYDRATES, 2G FAT

INGREDIENTS
- 250g // 9oz cooked beetroot
- 100g // 3 ½oz canned lentils
- 1 small apple, peeled and chopped
- 1 garlic clove, crushed
- 1 tsp onion seeds (nigella), plus extra to serve
- 250ml // 1 cup vegetable stock

INSTRUCTIONS
1. Tip the beetroot, lentils, apple, garlic, onion seeds and vegetable stock into the soup maker and set the smooth function.
2. Season to taste, and serve with the extra onion seeds scattered over.

BUTTERNUT SQUASH AND SWEET POTATO SOUP

This recipe is hearty, low in calories, and is a great way to use up leftover potatoes.

SERVES 6
PER SERVING: 89 CALORIES, 1.6G PROTEIN, 22.6G CARBOHYDRATES, 0.1G FAT

INGREDIENTS
- 300g // 10oz sweet potatoes, chopped
- 300g // 10oz butternut squash
- 1 tbsp chopped parsley
- Pinch salt
- Vegetable stock cube
- Hot water

INSTRUCTIONS
1. Chop up the vegetables, and put the vegetables, stock cube, and pinch of salt in the soup maker.
2. Add water to the MAX line and set the soup maker to smooth.
3. Serve with a sprinkling of parsley.

CARROT AND GINGER SOUP

Carrots make for a great soup, and when combined with ginger, you can create a wonderfully warming soup.

SERVES 4-6
PER SERVING: 140 CALORIES, 2.6G PROTEIN, 17.2G CARBOHYDRATES, 7.2G FAT

INGREDIENTS
- 500g // 17½oz carrots, chopped
- 150g // 5¼oz onion, sliced
- About 3-4 inches ginger, peeled and chopped
- 1 tsp salt
- 1L // 4 cups vegetable stock
- Peppercorns to garnish

INSTRUCTIONS
1. Add all the ingredients except the peppercorns to the soup maker and run on smooth.
2. Serve immediately and garnish with the peppercorns.

Dessert and drinks

At the end of a long day when you just want something sweet to follow dinner, you can whip up something delicious and sweet with our soup maker dessert and drink ideas.

RASPBERRY AND CHOCOLATE SOUP

This simple dessert recipe is packed with flavour that the whole family will love.

SERVES 3
PER SERVING: 535 CALORIES, 4.8G PROTEIN, 52.9G CARBOHYDRATES, 36.1G FAT

INGREDIENTS
- 400g // 14oz can of coconut milk
- 250ml // 1 cup cold water
- 200g // 7oz frozen raspberries
- 60ml // ¼ cup maple syrup
- 50g // 1¾oz dark chocolate
- 2 tsp vanilla extract
- Pinch of sea salt

INSTRUCTIONS
1. Add all the ingredients to the soup maker and run the smooth soup programme. Remove the lid and leave the mix to cool for a few minutes.
2. Pass the soup through a fine sieve to remove any raspberry seeds, and serve with raspberries, chocolate curls or a dollop of yoghurt.

COCONUT CUSTARD

This coconut custard recipe is gluten free and so easy to make.

SERVES 4
PER SERVING: 396 CALORIES, 5.7G PROTEIN, 31.6G CARBOHYDRATES, 29.5G FAT

INGREDIENTS

- 400g // 14oz can of coconut milk
- 5 egg yolks
- 60ml // ¼ cup agave nectar
- 60g // 2oz tapioca starch
- 1 tbsp vanilla

INSTRUCTIONS

1. Add all the ingredients to the soup maker. Secure the lid shut and select the blend function on a low speed. Allow to blend for 1 minute.

2. Select the cook function and medium temperature (or soup function on smooth) and cook for ten minutes. Then, cook for a further ten minutes on high. Make sure that you either pulse the mix or stop the cycle to stir the custard every 5 minutes.

3. Stop the cook function and pulse the custard for 10 seconds. Serve immediately.

(PROTEIN PUDDINGS)

Choose from three different flavours depending on your own preference for this delicious protein pudding.

SERVES 2
PER SERVING: 281 CALORIES, 21.5G PROTEIN, 19.9G CARBOHYDRATES, 13.1 G FAT

INGREDIENTS
- 400ml // 1½ cups water or milk
- 30g // 1oz whey protein powder
- 2 tbsp chia seeds
- For a vanilla pudding, add 1tsp vanilla extract
- For a chocolate pudding, add 1tbsp cocoa powder
- For a salted caramel pudding, add 2tbsp caramel syrup with ½ tsp salt

INSTRUCTIONS
1. Add all the ingredients for your desired flavour to the soup maker.
2. Select the dessert function.
3. Place into bowls or jars and allow to set in the fridge for an hour before serving.

COCONUT AND PINEAPPLE SORBET

This refreshing dessert is so easy to make and just needs six ingredients.

SERVES 4
PER SERVING: 269 CALORIES, 2.6G PROTEIN, 35.8G CARBOHYDRATES, 15.4 G FAT

INGREDIENTS

- 400g // 14oz frozen pineapple chunks
- 2 small frozen ripe bananas
- 2 tbsp fresh lime juice
- 250ml // 1 cup light coconut milk
- 2 tbsp agave nectar
- 1 tsp grated fresh ginger

INSTRUCTIONS

1. Place all the ingredients in the soup maker in the order listed.
2. Select the dessert function.
3. Serve immediately.

CUCUMBER AND MINT REFRESHER

This refreshing drink uses ginger ale as a base to make this recipe even easier.

SERVES 2
PER SERVING: 110 CALORIES, 1G PROTEIN, 28.1G CARBOHYDRATES, 0.2G FAT

INGREDIENTS
- 1/2 cucumber
- 6 mint leaves
- 500ml ginger ale
- Juice from 1 lime

INSTRUCTIONS
1. Add all the ingredients to the soup maker.
2. Blend on the manual setting until smooth, around 10-20 seconds.
3. Serve over ice.

(EGGNOG)

This festive drink can be whipped up in no time in your trusty soup maker.

SERVES 6
PER SERVING: 467 CALORIES, 10G PROTEIN, 39.8G CARBOHYDRATES, 23.5G FAT

INGREDIENTS
+ 6 egg yolks
+ 400g // 14oz tin sweetened condensed milk
+ 200g // 7oz heavy cream
+ 250ml // 1 cup milk
+ 150ml // ¾ cup spiced rum
+ Seeds from 1 vanilla pod

INSTRUCTIONS
1. Add all ingredients except rum to the blender jug.
2. Secure the lid and select the pulse function to combine all ingredients.
3. Select the sauce function.
4. Once cooking is complete, run the mixture through a strainer to remove any lumps.
5. Stir in the rum and serve either warm or chilled.

PEANUT BUTTER HOT CHOCOLATE

This hot chocolate is a great winter warmer for peanut butter lovers.

SERVES 2
PER SERVING: 467 CALORIES, 10G PROTEIN, 39.8G CARBOHYDRATES, 23.5G FAT

INGREDIENTS
- 750ml // 2 cups milk
- 250ml // 1 cup cream
- 250g // 8¾oz milk chocolate chips
- 4 tbsp smooth peanut butter

INSTRUCTIONS
1. Place milk, single cream, chocolate chips, and peanut butter in the jug.
2. Select the medium temperature function and cook for 20 minutes.
3. Pulse every 5 minutes during cooking.
4. Garnish with marshmallows or chocolate syrup as desired.

Disclaimer

This book contains opinions and ideas of the author and is meant to teach the reader informative and helpful knowledge while due care should be taken by the user in the application of the information provided. The instructions and strategies are possibly not right for every reader and there is no guarantee that they work for everyone. Using this book and implementing the information/recipes therein contained is explicitly your own responsibility and risk. This work with all its contents, does not guarantee correctness, completion, quality or correctness of the provided information. Misinformation or misprints cannot be completely eliminated.

Printed in Great Britain
by Amazon